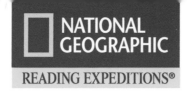

NATIONAL GEOGRAPHIC

READING EXPEDITIONS®

W9-AYG-074

KIDS AROUND THE WORLD

Maasai Dreamer

A Story from Kenya

By Adrienne Frater
Illustrated by Rick Powell

PICTURE CREDITS
3-7, 45-48 (borders) © MedioImages/Getty
Images; 6 Mapping Specialists, Ltd.; 7 (top)
© Tim Davis/Corbis; 7 (center) © Corbis; 7
(bottom) © Jim Zuckerman/Corbis; 45 ©
Martin Harvey/Getty Images; 46 (top) © W.
Perry Conway/Corbis; 46 (bottom) © Anthony
Bannister/Gallo Images/Corbis; 48 © Eric
Wheater/Lonely Planet Images (inset), © Gallo
Images/Corbis (background).

**PUBLISHED BY THE NATIONAL
GEOGRAPHIC SOCIETY**
Produced through the worldwide resources
of the National Geographic Society, John M.
Fahey, Jr., President and Chief Executive
Officer; Gilbert M. Grosvenor, Chairman of
the Board.

**PREPARED BY NATIONAL GEOGRAPHIC
SCHOOL PUBLISHING**
Sheron Long, Chief Executive Officer; Samuel
Gesumaria, President; Francis Downey, Vice
President and Publisher; Richard Easby,
Editorial Manager; Anne M. Stone, Editor;
Margaret Sidlosky, Director of Design and
Illustrations; Jim Hiscott, Design Manager;
Cynthia Olson, Ruth Ann Thompson, Art
Directors; Matt Wascavage, Director of
Publishing Services; Lisa Pergolizzi,
Production Manager.

MANUFACTURING AND QUALITY CONTROL
Christopher A. Liedel, Chief Financial Officer;
Phillip L. Schlosser, Vice President; Clifton M.
Brown III, Director.

CONSULTANT
Mary Anne Wengel

BOOK DESIGN
Steve Curtis Design, Inc.

Published by the National Geographic Society
1145 17th Street N.W.
Washington, D.C. 20036-4688

Product #4U1005106
ISBN: 978-1-4263-5099-3

Printed in Mexico.

15 14 13
10 9 8 7 6 5 4

Contents

Kenya

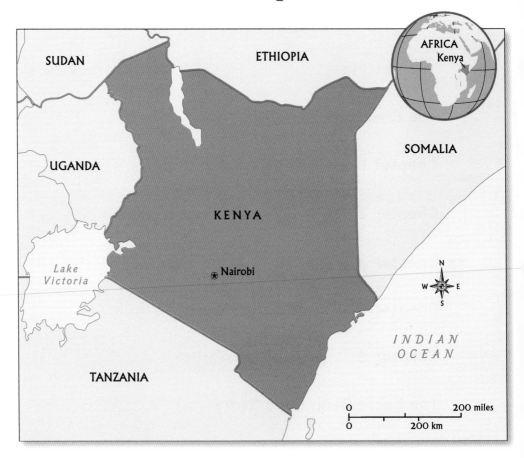

enya is a country on the eastern coast of Africa. It is about the size of Texas. Its capital is Nairobi. Kenya is surrounded by land to the north, west, and south. To the east lies the Indian Ocean. The head of Kenya's government is the president. Kenya elects a new president every five years.

Geography

Near the ocean, Kenya is mostly flat. It has lowlands and plains. The country also has two big mountain ranges. In the southwest, Kenya borders a large lake.

Climate

The weather in Kenya is often hot. The coast gets plenty of rain. But Kenya's plains are dry most of the year. Lack of rain is a big problem in these areas.

People

Kenya is home to 40 tribes. A tribe is a group of people with the same culture. The Maasai are one of these tribes. Many people in Kenya live in rural villages. Others live in cities such as Nairobi.

Maasai Dreamer

Atika

Atika (pronounced eye-TEE-ka) is a girl living in Kenya. She is a member of the Maasai tribe. She dreams that her school will build a well someday.

Saisa

Saisa (sa-EH-sa) is Atika's half brother. He helps herd animals after school.

Tumpe

Tumpe (TOOM-bay) is Atika's best friend. She and Atika are in the same class at school.

Kakuta

Kakuta (ka-KOO-ta) is Atika's older brother. He has an idea that might solve the school's well problem.

Emma

Emma is a visitor from Australia. She builds wells for a living. She may have some advice about a well for the school.

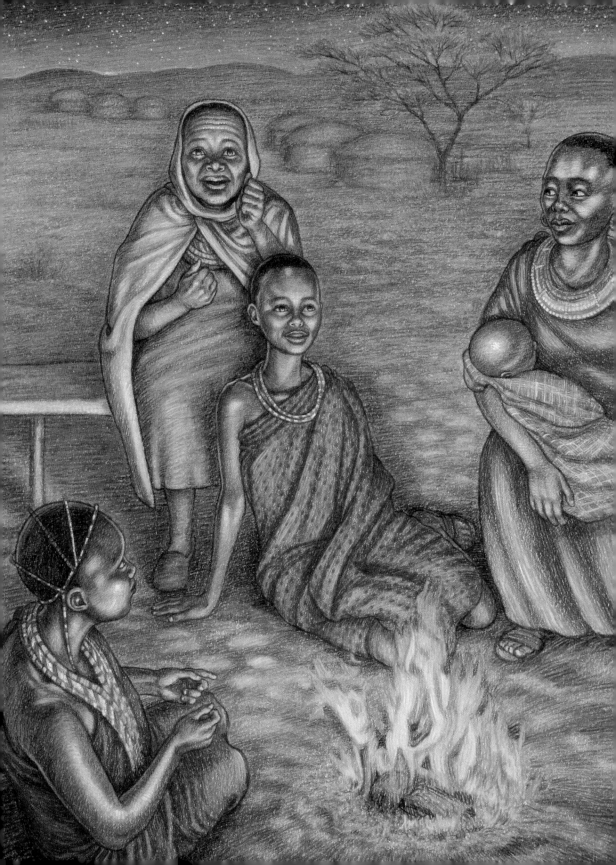

CHAPTER ONE

A Year of Drought

Atika leaned back against her grandmother's legs. Six women sat in a circle around the fire. Some nursed babies, while others watched the children play. Firelight shone on the bead necklaces around the women's necks. The black sky glittered with stars.

"Atika, Atika," her half brother Saisa called. "Come and play hide and seek." But Atika didn't answer. She pulled her robe more tightly around her chest.

"It's time for a story, Grandmother," she said.

"There once lived a hyena and a hare," began Grandmother. "Together they owned a great number of cows. Then one by one, the cows began to disappear. The hare suspected the hyena was eating them. After much thought, he came up with a plan. He lit a big fire. Then he suggested that they take turns jumping over it. The one with a cow in its belly would surely fall in."

The other children left their games and gathered around to hear the end of the story.

"The hare jumped safely across the fire," continued Grandmother. "But the hyena's belly was so full that she fell into the flames. The hare took great care of the cows that were left, for the rest of his days."

Atika shivered. She looked at their own cows, safe inside their strong pen of sticks. They were so thin that she could count their ribs. Her family needed the cows for food and drink. If a wild animal took one of them, it would be the end of the world.

For a time, nobody spoke. Even the animals were silent. Then, as Saisa stirred the fire with a stick, a distant lion roared.

"It's time for bed. You have school tomorrow," said Grandmother. The children scattered like dust in a storm.

Atika shared her cowhide sleeping mat with her younger sister. She cuddled close. The lion was still roaring, but farther away now. Atika stared up at the round roof of their hut. She thought about school the next day and playing with her best friend. She thought about her older brother at school in the city. Then, as she always did, Atika thought about rain. She hoped it would come soon. Suddenly, her eyelids became so heavy, they fell shut.

The next morning, Atika heard her mother moving around before it was light. She ran out to greet the African sun. First a strip of gold lit the bottom of the sky. Then the rest of the sky turned red. Atika ran across to the goats. She laid her head on the skinniest goat's ribs. She began squirting milk into the bowl. As she milked the goats, she gathered the colors in her head. The green of the flat-topped acacia trees. The row of

purple hills. The women's blue shadows as they bent to milk the cows. Early morning was the best part of Atika's day.

The sun was still low in the sky when the children set out on their long walk to school. Atika and Saisa were lucky. They had sandals made from car tires. Some children had no shoes. They had to stop now and then to pull thorns from their feet.

Saisa ran ahead with his friends. He was a year younger than his half sister. He had been born in the year of the big rain. Atika was jealous. She had been born in a drought year. If there was something she loved more than anything in the world, it was rain.

Each day as she walked to school, Atika would search the sky for dark clouds. It hadn't rained for over a year now. The land was parched and dry. If the rains didn't come soon, their animals might die. If their animals died, what would they eat? How would they pay for school? Atika walked a little faster. With every step, she kicked up a cloud of red dust.

Atika had been walking for an hour now. She still couldn't see the roof of their school. Dry grass scratched her ankles. She snapped a twig from a tree and cleaned her teeth. Where were all the zebras, giraffes, and gazelles? Soon the wild animals would have to leave the nearby **game park** to search for water. The animals were probably just as thirsty as she was.

After walking another half hour, Atika heard joyful shouts and screams. She had arrived at school at last. Atika had time to brush the dust from her uniform and greet her friend Tumpe. Then the bell rang. Atika, Tumpe, and Saisa were in the same class. They were proud of their school. It had three classrooms made of mud bricks. It had open windows and an open door, so the breeze could blow through.

Everyone from the nearby Maasai villages had helped build the school. Even the warriors had taken off their fancy bead necklaces and headgear to help make the bricks. Before the

game park – a wilderness area where people can watch wild animals

school was built, the children had lessons under a giant acacia tree. They sat on rocks and drew letters in the sand with sticks. The only thing their new school didn't have was a well. Every drop of water they used for drinking and cooking had to be carried a long distance.

The first lesson of the day was language skills. Atika had been at school for several years already. By now she could speak some Swahili and English, as well as her own language, Maa.

"I have a surprise," her teacher said. "Today we have a visitor from Australia."

The children's eyes grew very large. Atika and Tumpe sat perfectly still at the wooden desk they shared. Each girl knew what the other was thinking. They'd seen outsiders before, but had never met one. This woman had hair the color of corn. Her eyes were the same blue as the beads in Atika's mother's wedding necklace. Atika was surprised. The woman's skin was so much paler than hers. The children sat very quietly waiting for her to speak.

"Good morning, boys and girls," the visitor said. "My name is Emma."

The children could speak only a little English. But they understood most of what Emma said. She showed them pictures of Australia. She said her country was a little like Kenya. She showed a picture of her house. It was so big, the children thought it was a school.

Next she showed a picture of an animal called a kangaroo. It looked rather strange. It hopped on two large feet and carried its baby in a pocket on its belly. Then Emma left to speak to the students in the next classroom.

CHAPTER TWO

Waiting for Rain

During math Atika listened without hearing. She copied numbers from the blackboard without seeing. Her head buzzed with the new things she had heard.

At lunchtime, Saisa said that Emma was so light-skinned that she'd burn in the African sun. "She has a hat," said Tumpe in between mouthfuls of beans. She watched their visitor walk around the school grounds. "And she's wearing dark glasses."

After they had eaten, the two girls walked over to Emma. It was their turn to water the school garden. But today the plants could wait. Atika and Tumpe had something much more important to do.

"Excuse me," said Tumpe in English. "Are your cattle well?"

Emma smiled and took off her dark glasses. "I don't have any cows," she said. "I live in the city." She smiled again, and this time the girls smiled back. "I'm an environmental engineer," she told them. "But right now I'm on vacation."

"What is an environmental engineer?" The new words felt strange on Atika's tongue.

"I work with water," said Emma. "In some places in Australia, it hardly ever rains. So we build wells. We pump water from under the ground, the same as you do here." As Emma talked, she drew pictures in the sand.

"Can I touch your earrings?" asked Tumpe. Emma's earrings were made of clear blue stones that matched her eyes.

"My mother makes necklaces," Tumpe said. "So does Atika's."

"I'd love to see them," said Emma.

The afternoon passed very slowly. As it grew hotter, the students became thirsty. Saisa was pleased when Olurie, a Maasai elder, took them outside to talk about hunting lions. Storytelling was the best part of Saisa's day.

Olurie was tall and slim. His head was shaved. Heavy metal earrings had stretched a hole in his earlobes. Another pair of earrings hung from the top of each ear. They were threaded with red, blue, and green beads. Olurie wore two beaded armbands which his father had given him. His robe was tied over one shoulder, and he was holding a carved stick.

Saisa's eyes glittered as Olurie described his first lion hunt. He told the children how he had hunted down a lion. It had been after their cattle. He explained how his first kill had proved he was a real warrior. Olurie put on a lion-mane headdress and paraded around. Then the bell rang to mark the end of school.

The sun was low as Atika and Saisa reached their village. Although they were tired and hungry, they each had chores to do. Saisa had to help herd the animals. He ran another five miles until he reached the warriors. They were guarding the cows and goats. "It's so dry," said one of the warriors. "We had to go much farther today to find enough grass." Saisa knew the warriors were worried about drought.

Atika's chore was to fetch water from the village well. She pumped the water into a tin bucket, which she carried on her head. Then she took her young sister outside to play house. They arranged sticks in a circle and stuffed them with mud and straw. They smoothed animal dung onto the tiny roof. The house looked exactly like theirs, only smaller.

While Atika was playing, she thought about telling a story that night. She would tell everyone about Emma. She would tell them that Emma wanted to see the women's beadwork.

The sun slipped behind the hills, Atika hoisted her little sister onto her back. They returned for their meal.

There was silence around the cooking fire. The night air felt heavy. Atika hoped it was heavy with rain. She knew if the rains didn't come soon, they would have to leave their village to search for grass for the animals. The last time this had happened, Atika was very small. She remembered walking long distances over dry, dusty ground. She remembered how happy she had felt when the rains finally came.

"No," she decided. "People are too worried about the drought to listen to stories tonight. Emma's story can wait."

Atika lay on her sleeping mat and thought about her day. She thought about Emma and the work she did. She thought some more about rain. If it rained this week, they wouldn't have to leave. Her older brother Kakuta came home from school on Saturday. They'd run to the waterhole and watch the wild animals drink.

CHAPTER THREE

If Only!

By the end of the week the children had stopped watering the school garden. They saved the water for cooking and drinking.

The school had no well. So each family had to provide three gallons of water a week for each child. Some mothers carried the water in large plastic containers strapped to their heads. Atika's mother was lucky. Their village had a donkey to help her carry the heavy containers. She brought water every Friday.

When she hadn't arrived by recess, Atika grew worried. Was something wrong? Had the elephants trampled the fence? Was somebody injured? Had a cow fallen ill?

When the boys began playing soccer, Atika didn't watch with the others. The boys played with a ball made from melted plastic bags. The ball was so light, the wind sometimes snatched it away. Tumpe cheered as Saisa scored a goal. But Atika didn't hear. She was standing on the top branch of the acacia tree searching for her mother. By the time recess ended, her mother had still not appeared.

"Atika," said her teacher during class. He had drawn different grasses on the blackboard. He was explaining which grass grew where. "Atika, stop dreaming."

Atika's mother arrived just as the students were eating their lunch. "The pump broke," she said. "I had to go the next village to fetch water." She looked tired.

Atika helped her mother pour the precious water into the school tank. The tank was made from mud bricks and lined with black plastic. It sat right outside the kitchen door.

"If only our school had its own well," thought Atika. "If only our village had a new pump. If only the rains would come soon. If only I could could do something to help!"

Then Atika remembered that tomorrow was the first day of school vacation. Kakuta was coming home. He was the first boy in their village to go away to school in Nairobi. The other boys his age helped with the cattle. Then they became warriors.

The villagers were proud that Kakuta was so good at his studies. They had all helped pay for his school uniform and fees. This was his first visit home.

Atika knew it took all night for the bus to travel from Nairobi. The bus would have bumped and bounced along the lumpy dirt roads. Atika sighed. She was sure Kakuta would be too tired to answer any questions.

After she milked the goats and gathered the firewood next morning, Atika went walking. She saw giraffes in the distance. She took her young sister to watch them.

The giraffes were so tall they had to bend their necks to nibble the leaves. "Why are they so fussy?" asked her sister. "Why do they eat only a little from each tree?"

"Once they start eating, the tree pumps a nasty taste into its leaves," explained Atika. "So then they move on to another tree."

A little farther on they met a herd of zebras. The heat haze rippled their stripes. The zebras stopped at a patch of bare ground and rolled in the dust. The two girls stood very still, watching. Atika knew that each zebra had its own special pattern of stripes. If she were a zebra, she'd have to remember these patterns. They told which zebra was which. She was so busy thinking about this that she didn't notice the changing sky.

Her sister tugged Atika's robe. She pointed to the fat, black clouds. One cloud rose above another. A cloud mountain grew in the sky. The giraffes stretched their necks and sniffed the air. Then the girls spotted the shape of a tall man.

"Kakuta!" called Atika, as lightning flashed.

The two sisters ran toward their brother. A strong wind swept the rain toward them. Atika heard its roar before it arrived. Then fat raindrops poured from the sky.

Kakuta was taller than Atika remembered. His white school shirt stuck to his skin. He grinned as his two sisters danced in the rain.

That night the warriors killed a goat to celebrate Kakuta's homecoming. Everyone enjoyed the tasty goat stew. Kakuta was tired from his journey. But he stayed up to watch the warriors dance in the rain. As they jumped higher and higher, his grin grew wider and wider. Soon he and the younger boys joined in the dancing. Kakuta gave one last mighty leap. The villagers knew he was glad to be home.

CHAPTER FOUR

A Walk to the Waterhole

It didn't rain for just one or two days. It rained all that week. It looked like it would rain all the next week as well. Each day, Atika rejoiced at the sound of the rain. Just as the new grasses were growing, she felt she was growing too.

It was the third day of vacation before Kakuta and Atika were alone. "Why are you singing?" he asked, when she'd finished milking the goats.

"I always sing to the goats," explained Atika. "They give more milk that way. But let's not talk about the goats. Tell me about school," she said as she carried the milk inside. "Where do you sleep? Are there any other Maasai? Are there girls at your school? Do you have water taps? Does your school have a well?"

Kakuta laughed. It was a deeper laugh than Atika remembered. "Let's walk to the waterhole," he said. "Let's watch the wild animals drink."

Atika loved walking in the rain, but Kakuta didn't. He ran from tree to tree. Under each tree, he answered one of his sister's questions.

Under the first tree, Atika learned that twenty boys slept in each room. "They're called **dormitories,**" said Kakuta. "But we call them dorms. I'm in the hippo dorm." Atika stared at a cloud of white butterflies floating above a carpet of purple flowers. She tried to picture her brother sleeping in his hippo dorm.

Under the next tree, Atika learned that each dorm had three lightbulbs. "And taps, do you have any taps? And a well, do you have a well?"

"Of course we have taps. The school water travels through pipes."

Atika yanked her brother from under the tree. She dragged him toward the waterhole.

dormitory – a large room where many people sleep

"Of course we have taps," she mimicked. "What do you mean by of course? If we had one tap in our school, we'd be the luckiest school in the world!"

Her question was interrupted by a loud trumpeting sound. Atika and Kakuta stood very still. They watched a herd of elephants approach the waterhole.

The elephants ran to the edge, then spread their ears and froze. It was like they were following secret instructions. Suddenly their ears flopped back down. They charged into the muddy water. They drank first, then squirted each other and bathed.

"We used to drink this water once," said Kakuta. "Before we had a well, we had to share the water with the animals."

Atika and Kakuta watched the rhinos arrive next, then more zebras and wildebeests. Animal tracks led into and out of the waterhole. So many animals had drunk there since the rains began! There were birds too. Some were swimming. Others were flying high overhead.

"It reminds me of assembly at school," said Kakuta. "So many people from so many tribes."

"Are there many Maasai in your school?" asked Atika.

"There are three in my class, but they don't live with us in the dorms. They live in town with their families."

A new thought leaped into Atika's mind. When Kakuta finished school, would he return to become a warrior like his brothers and cousins? Or would he stay and work in Nairobi and never come home?

"Kakuta," she said, pushing the thought away. "A visitor came to our school last week. She's from Australia, and she's an environmental engineer. She wants to visit our village to look at our beadwork."

"Mmmm," said Kakuta. "My friend's family has a beadwork shop inside one of the game parks. The tourists pay good money for Maasai beadwork. They take it back home to hang on their walls. When is your visitor going to come?"

"I'm not sure. I've been waiting to tell everyone about her visit, but the time never feels right."

That night Kakuta was the storyteller again. He told them some more about living

:y. "Nairobi is so crowded," he said.

ts are jam-packed with cars, buses,

es, bikes, and dogs. At night I have

to find any stars."

e told them about visiting the markets.

some pocket money at school," he said.

I raked leaves and milked the school

on my way to the bus station, I went

The Nairobi markets sell everything

ever want. But the smells are so strong

e you feel dizzy. And all the barking,

g, and honking hurts your ears."

a stopped talking and listened to the

listened to the *brrrr* of the crickets.

He listened to the bleating of the goats. "I love school," he said. "But I miss living here."

"Did you buy anything?" asked Saisa, eyeing Kakuta's bulging bag.

"Yes. I bought presents."

When he tossed the younger boys a real soccer ball, they shrieked like parrots. Atika and her sisters and half sisters each unwrapped a round shiny mirror. Kakuta had bought shells and purple cloth for the women. Then he visited the men's cooking fire and passed some bottles around.

"Honey beer?" asked his father.

"No," explained Kakuta. "Soda pop."

The men waited for Olurie to drink first.
The old man took a great swig. It fizzed and
bubbled up his nose.

"Tomorrow night," thought Atika. "I'll tell
them about Emma tomorrow night."

But tomorrow night was too late. In the
morning, just after Tumpe had arrived to visit,
Emma walked in with their teacher.

CHAPTER FIVE

Beads for Water

Atika felt terrible. "It's like I kept Emma a secret," she told Tumpe. She watched her teacher introduce Emma to the elders. Once the warriors reached a certain age, they became elders. It was their job to organize the villagers and give advice. Olurie leaned forward in his carved chair. He invited the visitors to stay and drink tea.

Atika helped the women boil milk and stir sugar into the tea. "Her name's Emma," Atika whispered to her mother. "She wants to see your beadwork."

After she drank tea, Emma inspected the women's beautiful bead collars and necklaces. "The green beads are grass. The blue beads are sky. The red is the color of our tribe." Atika was proud that she could explain this in English.

After that her teacher had to **translate.** The women showed Emma how different patterns had different meanings. Some meant you were married. Some were for warriors. Others were for elders.

"This is gorgeous," said Emma. She admired Atika's mother's wedding necklace. "How long did it take to make?"

"A month," Atika translated.

"Do you know where I might buy a necklace like this?" Emma asked.

"I could make you one," Atika translated for her mother. The other women looked thoughtful. Maybe they could sell beadwork as well. They knew that some villagers sold beadwork at roadside stalls. But the prices were poor. While the women were thinking, an idea jumped into Atika's head.

"You could sell your beadwork inside the game park," she said. "Then we could use the money to help pay for a school well. Just think

----

translate – to change words from one language to another

how much time you would save if you didn't have to carry water to school." Atika took a big breath and looked at Emma. "Emma knows all about wells. Maybe she could tell us what kind of well would be best."

There was silence for a time. Then Atika heard her teacher translating for Emma. Her teacher smiled. Emma smiled. The women smiled. They liked her idea. Grandmother nodded, then poured fresh cups of tea.

"Thank you," Emma said to the women. "Thank you," she said to the elders. Then she smiled at Atika and Tumpe as she left.

The weather was fine the day Kakuta put his uniform back on and set off for the bus. This time Atika got up before sunrise to walk with him. From time to time, Kakuta stopped to brush red clay from his pants. At school, dirt was frowned on. In his village, it was used for decoration. Kakuta shook his head. He'd just settled back into village life. Now it was time to change again. Sometimes he didn't know where he belonged.

"I've been thinking," Atika said, to the back of her brother's white shirt. "We could call the well project Beads for Water."

"That's good thinking," said Kakuta. "And I've been thinking about all of the other questions you asked me. Remember you asked if there are any girls at my school?"

"Are there?"

"Most of our students are boys, but there are a few girls. I think it's really important for girls to get a good education. I think you should be the next one from our village to go away to school."

This thought was so big, Atika said nothing for the next two miles. Kakuta was pleased with the silence. He knew he had planted the idea in Atika's mind. In time it would grow.

"About the well," he said some time later. "In science, we learned about using energy from the sun. It can be used to run machines. You know how our village water pump keeps breaking down? And you know how expensive it is to buy fuel? Maybe we could use sunshine to pump water for the school well."

Kakuta spent the rest of the walk answering his sister's eager questions. Then he boarded his bus and was gone.

Atika waved until the bus became as small as an ant. Then she began the long trudge home.

She was tired on her first day back at school. Her legs had walked a long way the day before. Her mind had traveled a long way too. But she wasn't too tired to talk about her plan. "Excuse me," she said to her teacher after lunch. "We need to talk some more about the well."

Her teacher listened to what she said and nodded. "We've already called a meeting for Saturday," he said. "And I like Kakuta's idea. I think a **solar-powered** well is just what we need."

---

solar-powered – using sunlight to make power

The meeting was held under the giant acacia tree. After much talking, the elders from the different villages agreed to start saving for a school well. "Now that our animals have more grass to eat, they give more milk," said one elder. "So maybe each village could donate a cow."

"The women plan to sell their beadwork inside the game park," said another elder. "They say they want the money they earn to go toward the school well."

Soon everyone was talking about the plan. During the next art lesson, the students made

two large BEADS FOR WATER signs. They hung one up on the school notice board. They planned to hang the other up inside the game park.

A few days later, Emma paid her last visit to the school. As she left, she handed the teacher a book.

"Inside is information about solar-powered wells," she said. "Good luck with your project. Please write and tell me how it goes." Sunlight danced on the beautiful blue necklace Emma had bought from Atika's mother.

Atika hummed as she walked home with Saisa and Tumpe. They'd had more rain since Kakuta left. The grass was now up to their knees. "It's all very well to dream," said Saisa. "But it will take forever to pay for this well."

"No it won't," said Tumpe. "I've made four wristbands already."

"And Olurie has met with the manager of the game park," said Atika. "He's agreed to let the women open a beadwork shop inside the tourist lodge."

Saisa snorted and ran ahead. Atika looked at Tumpe and rolled her eyes. Then she looked at the grassland, which seemed to go on forever. It was hard to imagine what lay on the other side. It was hard to imagine that Emma and Kakuta's world was so different from hers. Then Tumpe began running, so Atika ran too. She ran faster and faster, until the green grassland became a blur.

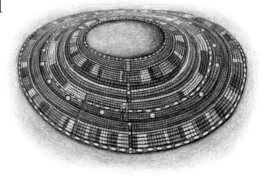

Maasai Culture

Atika and her family are fictional characters. That means they are made up. But many things about the story are true. Water is a concern for the Maasai. Cattle and goats are important in this culture. Beaded jewelry is a real Maasai tradition too.

The Water Supply

Finding safe drinking water is a big problem for the Maasai. Most Maasai do not have running water in their homes. They drink from rivers, streams, and waterholes. Some Maasai have access to wells. But they must often walk miles to get the water. When droughts come, finding water is even harder.

Herding

Cattle and goats are important to the Maasai. In fact, the Maasai believe a god gave cattle to their people. Cattle and goats supply meat, milk, and hides, or skins. The animals are a source of a family's wealth. Traditionally, the Maasai are herders. They travel from place to place with their animals, searching for food and water.

Maasai Beadwork

Maasai women are skilled at making jewelry. They are known for their beadwork. Bead colors and patterns have specific meanings. They can tell you about a person. For example, one pattern means that a woman is married. Another pattern tells you a man is a warrior.

Create a Travel Brochure

You read about a plan to raise money by selling Maasai jewelry to tourists in Kenya. Now help tourists learn about Kenya. Create a brochure that tells what people can see and do on their travels.

- Research at the library or online. Find out about festivals, food, and fun things to do.

- Decide what to show in your brochure. What is special about Kenya?

- Give each column a heading, such as "For Kids" or "What to See." Write a paragraph for each.

- Search for pictures of Kenya, or draw your own.

- Put your text and pictures together to make a brochure. Use the model below as an example.

For Kids	Festivals	What to See
	Food	

Read More About Other Cultures

Find and read more books about countries in Africa. As you read, think about these questions. They will help you understand more about this topic.

- What is life like in this country?
- What is special about this country?
- How is this country changing?
- What are people doing to keep their traditions alive?

SUGGESTED READING
Reading Expeditions
Communities Around the World:
Durban, South Africa

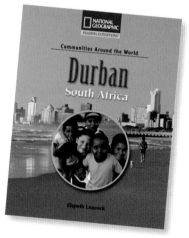